Reflections
From a Garden

by
Judy Carlson

Copyright © 2014 Judy Carlson

ISBN: 978-1-62646-909-9

All rights reserved. No part of this publication may be reproduced, stored in a retrieval system, or transmitted in any form or by any means, electronic, mechanical, recording or otherwise, without the prior written permission of the author.

Printed in the United States of America

Reflections
From a Garden

This book of reflection and healing is dedicated to
Ariel Arias
For believing in me.

In the Garden

Austin Miles, 1912

I come to the garden alone, While the dew is still on the roses;

And the voice I hear, falling on my ear,

The Son of God discloses.

He speaks, and the sound of His voice Is so sweet the birds hush their singing; And the melody that He gave to me Within my heart is ringing.

I'd stay in the garden with Him

Though the night around me be falling; But He bids me go through the voice of woe,

His voice to me is calling.

And He walks with me, and He talks with me, And He tells me I am His own;

And the joy we share as we tarry there None other has ever known.

This was the beginning of my garden.

You may be afraid of the challenge, but just do the first thing and the rest will follow.

The most difficult part of any journey is the first step.

When I received my diagnosis a few years ago I was full of fear and doubt that this thing, could be happening to me. But I read Psalm 139:14 and all the fear melted away.

I was encouraged to get a dog, and start a garden, walk and meditate and pray. I was determined to spend whatever time I had left growing and polishing my soul.

Instead of life gathering speed, I managed to slow down.

I planted 35 roses, and my son built me an arbor and potting table. My friend Rose gave me an old wooden chair to paint, and Coco and I spent almost all of our time outside.

I gave thanks with a grateful heart, took a deep breath and was still.

Sunshine Daydream

I come to the garden alone...
while the dew is still on the roses...

The sunrise holds the promise of many blessings. It is in our nature to work and be productive, to move. To be still and wholly enter the now takes practice. In the garden, it becomes easier to sit among the flowers, see their colors, and smell their fragrance, and to be grateful.

God the Lord has spoken and summoned the earth,
from the rising of the sun to it's setting.

Psalm 50:1

Neptune

And the voice I hear falling on my ear...

In the garden I wonder at the lavender color. I see and hear the bees come to drink the sweet fragrance. I hear the breeze rustle the leaves on the tree. I hear the birds happily singing, taking joy in being what God made them to be. The humming birds and the monarchs flutter by.

I look up and see the clouds drifting by against the beautiful blue of the Nevada sky. It makes me wonder what is beyond.

Fluffy white clouds are seen high above Neptune. Cloud shadows have not been seen on any other planet.

The heavens declare the Glory of God

Psalm 19:1

Opening Night

The Son of God discloses...

I believe that we are all given a moment, a time when we are prepared to receive, an opening night. Our God is outside of time, it's so easy to forget that. We are bound by the clock and schedules but He is forever in the moment.

When we stop, take a breath [Spiritus] see and feel Him all around us, He is with us.

> And behold, I am with you always,
> until the end of the age.
>
> Matthew 28:20

Sugar Moon

**He speaks and the sound of His voice,
Is so sweet the birds hush their singing**

Sugar Moon is a particularly delicate and beautiful rose. Its fragrance is indeed sweet and I also noticed in the garden it seemed more vulnerable. That may be a truth of nature, that the more beautiful and delicate, the more susceptible.

Its purity makes me think of children, innocent and joy filled.

Let the children come to me, and do not prevent them; for the kingdom of God belongs to such as these.

Luke 18:16

Double Delight

And the melody that He gave to me within my heart is ringing…

The white and red of this rose cannot help but take me to the purity of truth that is God, and the blood of the Lamb that is Jesus.

I hope you can grant me this reflection, if you are not a Christian. I do not seek to convince anyone of what is in my heart. I only wish to share with you where the beauty of my garden has taken me. The possibilities for everyone are as unique and diverse as life itself.

> I came so that you might have life and have it more abundantly.
>
> John 10:10

Let Freedom Ring

I'd stay in the garden with Him though the night around me is falling.

This Freedom rose is gorgeous. It grows tall and stately, proud and long stemmed. I think the way we are supposed to grow. Our gift of free will is our greatest gift after the gift of Faith. The choices that we make, make us who we become.

The reflections that I have taken from my garden have helped me to focus on what is lovely and true. I would stay in the garden with Coco all day until the night around us fell.

> Then Peter said to Jesus,
> Rabbi it is good that we are here!
> Let us make three tents.
>
> Matthew 17:4

Topsy Turvy

**But He bids me go; through the voice of woe
His voice to me is calling.**

This rose alters its appearance so much. When it buds it is mostly red but then opens to red, yellow and white. This rose calls me to move on, not to be stuck or too comfortable at one point in my life. Whether you respond to the voice of God or the universe the point of the journey is to keep moving. Life may at times seem topsy-turvy but all things work for good.

We know that all things work for good for those who love God, who are called according to His purpose.

Romans 8:28

About Face

And He walks with me and He talks to me...

Metanoia, or about face, is a changed mindset, a rebuilding or healing. In other words repentance. As this rose opens its shades run from bright orange to a creamy orange. The fragrance is even distinct. We burn brightly at our core and as we grow throughout our journey we mellow and learn, growing in grace and peace.

> All good giving and every perfect gift
> is from above coming down from the Father of Lights,
> with whom there is no shadow of turning.
>
> James 1:17

Secret

And He tells me that I am His own...

When we think of secrets we often fear they are a negative, but secrets in the garden are happy, lovely, delightful and inspirational things. The beauty that lies all around us, the beauty and truth that waits to be discovered just with a quiet look. The stimulation of all of our senses, making us fully alive and in the moment.

> My soul you knew full well when I was made in secret, when I was fashioned in the depths of the earth.
>
> Psalm 139:14

Coco Loco

And the joy we share as we tarry there none other has ever known..

This is such a unique rose. It buds perfectly as a mild chocolate brown and then opens in shades of light lavender. It is transformed. We too are transformed in life. We move through stages of dying and rising, discovering and letting go. If we tarry, even a little the rewards are huge. I do not suggest that a garden is a cure for what ails us, but I do recommend taking the time to see the beauty all around. It will bring you joy to connect.

> "Tarry with us, for it is nearly evening
> and the day is almost over."
> And it happened that while
> He was with them their eyes were opened.
>
> Luke 24: 29-31

Peace

I come to the Garden alone...

The name of this beautiful rose is self explanatory. I wish for all who read this little garden book, or even just pick it up and look at the pictures Peace, in your lives, hearts and souls.

I wish for you, Peace in your bodies. When we are ill, it is so important to think only positively. The beauty of the garden and these roses obviously distracted me from my own health issues and allowed me to appreciate beauty.

> And let the beauty of the Lord our God be upon us,
> and confirm for us the work of our hands;
> yes, confirm the work of our hands.
>
> Psalm 90:17

Show Biz

When the dew is still on the roses

This is a show-off little rose bush. There are always multiple clumps of roses. Most of the multiplying references in scripture of course come in Genesis. "Be fruitful and", "I will greatly", "men began to", "I will", and "make thee fruitful and multiply". The Creator was very busy for 6 days. He encoded His creation to repeat, to multiply. It was a gracious and generous act. I see in this the God of the second chances, and of course many more. Multiply your kindness, patience, fortitude, faith, gentleness and love. These are indeed the things that really matter, so show off.

> Now may the God who gives perseverance and encouragement grant you to be of the same mind.
>
> Romans 15:5

Old English

And the voice I hear falling on my ear..

I believe that God whispers our name into our soul as life begins. It is the most intimate of acts, sharing breath with us. But, we must spend time in the quiet to enter the soul where He is there, waiting.

Whoever has ears ought to hear what the Spirit says...
to him who overcomes...
I will give him a white stone, and a new name written on the stone which no one knows but he who receives it.

Revelation 2:17

Purple Tiger

**He speaks and the sound of His voice,
Is so sweet the birds hush their singing..**

The purple tiger of course makes me think of the roar of the tiger. It is a strong and bold rose. When I heard the roar at Niagara Falls I thought of the power of God. But in the garden surrounded by color, fragrance, bees, butterflies, and soft breezes I come to the quiet.

Go outside and stand on the mountain.
A strong and heavy wind was rending the mountain and crushing rocks, but the Lord was not in the wind...
there was an earthquake, but the Lord was not in the earthquake. After the earthquake there was a fire,
but the Lord was not in the fire.
After the fire there was a tiny whispering sound.

1 Kings 19:11

Winchester Cathedral

And the melody that He gave to me within my heart is ringing...

This lovely old English rose is named after a cathedral with bells that sing out to all around. Our God dwells within praises, not because He is in need of validation, but because we are made whole in the process. Ring out your joy to the Lord, in praise of God's mercy.

The just man sings and rejoices.

Proverbs 29:6

Angel Face

I'd stay in the garden with Him

Angels are first spoken of in Genesis, and end in Revelation. So from the beginning, to the end, I like to think that they are all around us sharing messages, protecting us, comforting us, and accompanying us on our journey through life.

In scripture we find that Jesus is ministered to by angels… in the desert, but also a garden.

And to strengthen Him
an angel from heaven appeared to Him

Luke 22:43

Easy Does It

But He bids me go...

It is easy to stay in the garden. The colors are magnificent, the scent of the roses floats by, and I hear a buzz, look up and see a hummingbird checking me out. Have you ever been a witness to six or eight finches splashing about having a group bath? It is pure and simple joy to watch.

But…easy does it, is right…there are things waiting inside to be done. There is a family coming home soon with "what's for dinner," on their lips.

So…He bids me go…

> Go, therefore, and make disciples of all nations.
> Matthew 28:19

Ginger Snap

His voice to me is calling...

Ginger means pure, and ginger snap is pure beauty. It is full of color and curl and delightful to look at. It is a prolific rose always full of blossoms. Each one of these roses is unique, as we all are. I found this interesting when I looked pure up in the dictionary one of the definitions was 'producing offspring which do not vary from the type of parent with respect to character.'

If we can be prolific in our lives , let us strive to be pure in heart.

Blessed are the pure in heart for they will see God.

Matthew 5:8

Gemini

And He walks with me and He talks with me...

Gemini buds open to reveal double blossoms of cream and coral, double, two by two. I believe that we were never meant to be solitary. There is never one cloud in the sky, one tree in the forest, or one mountain peak claiming to be a range. Even when we think we are alone we are surrounded by angels and so great a cloud of witnesses. Whether it is a loving spouse, a mate, a great friend, a kitty cuddled on your lap or a faithful dog by your side, you are never really alone.

And He summoned the twelve
and began to send them out two by two.

Mark 6:7

And He tells me that I am His own...

The name Elizabeth is Hebrew for 'Oath of God.'

It is that God thought of us, that we exist at all. He conceived of us before we were conceived in our mothers. There is much meaning in a name. Throughout scripture names matter and are sometimes changed to illustrate the transformation of the person. Abram to Abraham, Simon to Peter, and Sarai to Sarah.

I will never forget you my people,
I have carved you on the palm of my hand.

Isaiah 49:16

Marmalade Skies

And the joy we share...

Earlier when I spoke of the Nevada night sky I said that stars are for those who look up. We have eyes to see and ears to hear but sometimes we move too quickly to appreciate what our senses detect. I told of sunsets with colors of pink and gold and yellow and yes oranges too. This rose of marmalade skies makes me think of another sky event…

And you shall see the Son of Man
sitting at the right hand of power,
and coming with the clouds of heaven.

Matthew 26:64

Stainless Steel

I come to the garden...

If you have ever battled with any description of illness, you may guess where I am going with stainless steel.

I believe every person has an untapped reservoir of strength and courage. This rose reminds me of that truth.

I think the most difficult part for me was accepting that I had a potentially serious health problem.

Once I found Psalm 139:14 in my bible I knew that I was indeed in God's hands. I surrendered to the path before me.

> And it came about,
> when the days were approaching for
> His ascension, that He set His face like flint to go to Jerusalem.
>
> Luke 9:51

Salt Grass

This is obviously not one of my roses, but I feel it should be featured not just as part of any Nevada garden, but as a true survivor.

These blades of grass have pushed their way through asphalt. These slender, sticks of grass, one at a time have made their way through tar and rock.

Tenacious… persistent.

> I have fought the good fight,
> I have finished the course,
> I have kept the faith
>
> 2 Timothy 4:7

Wild Blue Yonder

Up, up and away! The Nevada sky is so blue and beautiful. It is easy to sit and admire the sunrises and sunsets. Our skies are almost always clear but in the spring and fall we can have a special treat of those wispy cirrus clouds in the evening. When the sun goes down they light up with pink, and yellow, and gold.

It is especially gorgeous at night as we have such clear dark skies. The stars are for those who look up and I never fail to remember that.

I have wanted to share these garden reflections with you who love the beauty that God has provided, for those of us who garden or who battle illness or disease, and all Christians who like me can see the glory of God all around.

When I began to take pictures of my roses it was just to capture a moment in time when they looked perfect for me. Then like anyone who has something of wonder you want to share it, so I put my garden on Facebook.

I am currently in my sixties, and have not exactly escaped a diagnosis or two. When I began to write my reflections I was happily overcoming something called Polycythemia Vera. Now, I have moved on to other challenges.

Please don't think I look for sympathy. Remember, I said our lives are full of dying and rising moments and I know we are all in God's loving hands. When Jesus was in the garden He prayed to have His cup pass over. I will follow His example, but I will also surrender to the Father's will.

My rose garden has been a joy filled journey. The high desert of Nevada is not exactly the most hospitable environment for roses. That makes the challenge all the more rewarding. I pray and wish for you who read and enjoy this little book that life's challenges will never get you down. That you will go into the quiet, reach deep inside to find hope and live it everyday.